Easy Fish Cookbook

By CARLA HUTSON

Copyright 2024 By CARLA HUTSON. All rights reserved.

No part of this book may be reproduced in any form or by any electronic or mechanical means, including information storage and retrieval systems, without written permission from the author, except for the use of brief quotations in a book review.

Table of Contents

Mediterranean Fish Soup 5

Creamy Fish Chowder 7

Thai Coconut Fish Soup... 9

Italian Fish and Vegetable Soup 11

Spicy Fish Soup 13

Baked Lemon Garlic Tilapia.. 15

Simple Grilled Salmon.. 17

Easy Tuna Salad.. 19

Pan-Seared Cod with Butter Sauce 21

Honey Garlic Glazed Salmon 23

Baked Parmesan-Crusted Tilapia... 25

Cajun Blackened Fish Tacos... 27

Simple Baked Trout 29

Teriyaki Glazed Salmon 31

Quick Lemon Herb Grilled Swordfish.................................... 33

Grilled Lemon Herb Salmon... 34

Grilled Cajun Tilapia 36

Grilled Mahi Mahi with Mango Salsa 37

Grilled Swordfish Steaks with Rosemary and Garlic 39

Grilled Tuna Steaks with Soy and Ginger 41

Grilled Halibut with Basil Pesto 43

Grilled Trout with Lemon and Dill.. 44

Grilled Red Snapper with Garlic and Herbs 45

Grilled Sea Bass with Lemon Garlic Sauce............................ 47

Classic Southern Fried Catfish.. 49

Crispy Fried Tilapia 51

Beer-Battered Fish 53

Panko-Crusted Fried Cod.. 55

Fried Fish Tacos.. 57

Creamy Garlic Parmesan Fish 59

Tomato Basil Fish 61

Coconut Curry Fish.. 63

Lemon Butter Fish 65

Dijon Mustard Cream Fish... 67

Stuffed Salmon with Spinach and Cream Cheese............................. 69

Crab-Stuffed Flounder 71

Stuffed Trout with Lemon and Herbs 73

Shrimp-Stuffed Tilapia 75

Stuffed Haddock with Spinach and Feta.. 77

Steamed Ginger Soy Snapper 79

Maple Glazed Salmon.. 81

Pistachio-Crusted Cod 83

Moroccan Spiced Fish.. 85

Grilled Fish Tacos with Avocado Crema.. 87

Lemon Basil Baked Fish.. 89

Ginger Scallion Steamed Fish.. 90

Steamed Fish with Lemon and Herbs 92

Thai-Style Steamed Fish.. 94

Mediterranean Steamed Fish.. 96

Steamed Fish with Soy and Garlic... 98

Mediterranean Fish Soup

Mediterranean Fish Soup is a light yet flavorful dish inspired by the coastal flavors of the Mediterranean. The combination of fresh fish, tomatoes, and herbs creates a healthy and satisfying meal.

TOTAL TIME COOKING: 30 minutes

Ingredients:

- 1 lb white fish fillets (such as cod or halibut), cut into bite-sized pieces
- 2 tablespoons olive oil
- 1 onion, chopped
- 3 cloves garlic, minced
- 1 can (14 oz) diced tomatoes
- 4 cups fish or vegetable broth
- 1 teaspoon dried oregano
- 1/2 teaspoon dried thyme
- Salt and pepper, to taste
- 1/4 cup fresh parsley, chopped
- Lemon wedges, for serving

<u>Directions:</u>

1. Heat the olive oil in a large pot over medium heat.
2. Add the chopped onion and cook until softened.
3. Stir in the garlic and cook for 1 minute until fragrant.
4. Add the diced tomatoes, broth, oregano, and thyme. Bring to a simmer.
5. Add the fish pieces and season with salt and pepper.
6. Simmer for 10-12 minutes until the fish is cooked through and flakes easily.
7. Stir in the fresh parsley and serve with lemon wedges.

Creamy Fish Chowder

Creamy Fish Chowder is a rich and comforting soup that's perfect for cold days. The creamy broth is loaded with tender fish and potatoes, making it a hearty and satisfying meal.

TOTAL TIME COOKING: 35 minutes

Ingredients:

- 1 lb white fish fillets (such as cod or haddock), cut into bite-sized pieces
- 4 slices bacon, chopped
- 1 onion, chopped
- 2 cloves garlic, minced
- 2 potatoes, peeled and diced
- 3 cups fish or vegetable broth
- 1 cup heavy cream
- 1 bay leaf
- Salt and pepper, to taste
- Fresh parsley, chopped (optional)

Directions:

1. In a large pot, cook the chopped bacon over medium heat until crispy. Remove the bacon and set aside, leaving the drippings in the pot.
2. Add the chopped onion and cook until softened.
3. Stir in the garlic and cook for 1 minute until fragrant.
4. Add the diced potatoes, broth, and bay leaf. Bring to a simmer and cook for 10-12 minutes until the potatoes are tender.
5. Stir in the heavy cream and fish pieces, and season with salt and pepper.
6. Simmer for another 8-10 minutes until the fish is cooked through.
7. Remove the bay leaf, stir in the crispy bacon, and garnish with fresh parsley if desired.

Thai Coconut Fish Soup

Thai Coconut Fish Soup is a fragrant and flavorful dish that combines the creaminess of coconut milk with the zest of lime and spices. This soup is both comforting and exotic.

TOTAL TIME COOKING: 25 minutes

Ingredients:

- 1 lb white fish fillets (such as tilapia or snapper), cut into bite-sized pieces
- 1 tablespoon vegetable oil
- 2 cloves garlic, minced
- 1 tablespoon red curry paste
- 1 can (14 oz) coconut milk
- 2 cups fish or vegetable broth
- 1 tablespoon fish sauce
- Juice of 1 lime
- 1 red bell pepper, sliced
- Fresh cilantro, chopped
- Lime wedges, for serving

Directions:

1. Heat the vegetable oil in a large pot over medium heat.
2. Add the minced garlic and red curry paste, cooking for 1-2 minutes until fragrant.
3. Stir in the coconut milk, broth, fish sauce, and lime juice. Bring to a simmer.
4. Add the sliced red bell pepper and fish pieces to the pot.
5. Simmer for 10-12 minutes until the fish is cooked through and the bell pepper is tender.
6. Garnish with fresh cilantro and serve with lime wedges.

Italian Fish and Vegetable Soup

Italian Fish and Vegetable Soup is a hearty and healthy dish that's packed with vegetables and tender fish. This soup is perfect for a light yet satisfying meal.

TOTAL TIME COOKING: 30 minutes

Ingredients:

- 1 lb white fish fillets (such as haddock or cod), cut into bite-sized pieces
- 2 tablespoons olive oil
- 1 onion, chopped
- 2 cloves garlic, minced
- 2 carrots, sliced
- 2 celery stalks, sliced
- 1 can (14 oz) diced tomatoes
- 4 cups fish or vegetable broth
- 1 teaspoon dried basil
- 1 teaspoon dried oregano
- Salt and pepper, to taste
- Fresh basil, chopped (optional)

__Directions:__

1. Heat the olive oil in a large pot over medium heat.
2. Add the chopped onion, carrots, and celery, cooking until softened.
3. Stir in the garlic and cook for 1 minute until fragrant.
4. Add the diced tomatoes, broth, basil, and oregano. Bring to a simmer.
5. Add the fish pieces and season with salt and pepper.
6. Simmer for 10-12 minutes until the fish is cooked through and the vegetables are tender.
7. Garnish with fresh basil, if desired, and serve with crusty bread.

Spicy Fish Soup

Spicy Fish Soup is a bold and flavorful dish that's perfect for those who enjoy a bit of heat. The combination of spices and tender fish makes this soup a warming and satisfying meal.

TOTAL TIME COOKING: 25 minutes

Ingredients:

- 1 lb white fish fillets (such as tilapia or snapper), cut into bite-sized pieces
- 1 tablespoon olive oil
- 1 onion, chopped
- 3 cloves garlic, minced
- 1 teaspoon paprika
- 1/2 teaspoon cayenne pepper (adjust to taste)
- 1 can (14 oz) diced tomatoes
- 4 cups fish or vegetable broth
- 1 red bell pepper, chopped
- Salt and pepper, to taste
- Fresh cilantro or parsley, chopped (optional)

<u>Directions:</u>

1. Heat the olive oil in a large pot over medium heat.
2. Add the chopped onion and cook until softened.
3. Stir in the garlic, paprika, and cayenne pepper, cooking for 1 minute until fragrant.
4. Add the diced tomatoes, broth, and chopped red bell pepper. Bring to a simmer.
5. Add the fish pieces and season with salt and pepper.
6. Simmer for 10-12 minutes until the fish is cooked through and the bell pepper is tender.
7. Garnish with fresh cilantro or parsley, if desired, and serve hot.

Baked Lemon Garlic Tilapia

This Baked Lemon Garlic Tilapia is a quick and healthy meal that's perfect for busy weeknights. The fish is tender and flaky, with a bright lemony flavor and a hint of garlic. It pairs perfectly with a side of steamed vegetables or a fresh salad.

TOTAL TIME COOKING: 20 minutes

Ingredients:

1. 4 tilapia fillets
2. 2 tablespoons olive oil
3. 2 cloves garlic, minced
4. 1 lemon, sliced into rounds
5. Salt and pepper, to taste
6. Fresh parsley, chopped (optional)

Directions:

1. Preheat your oven to 400°F (200°C). Line a baking sheet with parchment paper.
2. Place the tilapia fillets on the prepared baking sheet.

3. Drizzle olive oil over the fillets and sprinkle minced garlic evenly on top.
4. Lay the lemon slices over the tilapia, then season with salt and pepper.
5. Bake for 10-12 minutes, or until the fish flakes easily with a fork.
6. Garnish with fresh parsley, if desired, and serve immediately.

Simple Grilled Salmon

This Simple Grilled Salmon recipe is ideal for summer barbecues or a quick weeknight dinner. The salmon is moist and flavorful, with a slightly smoky char from the grill.

TOTAL TIME COOKING: 15 minutes

Ingredients:

- 4 salmon fillets
- 2 tablespoons olive oil
- 1 tablespoon soy sauce
- 1 tablespoon honey
- 1 teaspoon Dijon mustard
- Salt and pepper, to taste
- Lemon wedges, for serving

Directions:

1. Preheat your grill to medium-high heat.
2. In a small bowl, whisk together the olive oil, soy sauce, honey, and Dijon mustard.
3. Brush the salmon fillets with the marinade, then season with salt and pepper.

4. Grill the salmon, skin-side down, for 4-6 minutes per side, depending on the thickness of the fillets.
5. Serve with lemon wedges and your favorite side dishes.

Easy Tuna Salad

This Easy Tuna Salad is a versatile recipe that can be served as a sandwich filling, a topping for salads, or a quick snack with crackers. It's light, refreshing, and packed with protein.

TOTAL TIME COOKING: 10 minutes

Ingredients:

- 2 cans of tuna, drained
- 1/4 cup mayonnaise
- 1 tablespoon Dijon mustard
- 1 tablespoon lemon juice
- 1 stalk celery, finely chopped
- 2 tablespoons red onion, finely chopped
- Salt and pepper, to taste
- Fresh dill, chopped (optional)

Directions:

1. In a large bowl, combine the drained tuna, mayonnaise, Dijon mustard, and lemon juice.

2. Add the chopped celery and red onion, and mix until well combined.
3. Season with salt and pepper, and add fresh dill if using.
4. Serve immediately or chill in the refrigerator until ready to use.

Pan-Seared Cod with Butter Sauce

This Pan-Seared Cod with Butter Sauce is a quick and delicious way to enjoy a healthy, light dinner. The buttery sauce complements the mild flavor of the cod perfectly.

TOTAL TIME COOKING: 15 minutes

Ingredients:

- 4 cod fillets
- 2 tablespoons olive oil
- 2 tablespoons butter
- 2 cloves garlic, minced
- Juice of 1 lemon
- Salt and pepper, to taste
- Fresh parsley, chopped (optional)

Directions:

1. Heat the olive oil in a large skillet over medium-high heat.
2. Season the cod fillets with salt and pepper, and add them to the skillet.

3. Cook the cod for 3-4 minutes on each side until golden brown and cooked through.
4. Remove the cod from the skillet and set aside.
5. In the same skillet, add the butter and garlic, cooking for about 1 minute until fragrant.
6. Stir in the lemon juice, and pour the sauce over the cod fillets.
7. Garnish with parsley, if desired, and serve immediately.

Honey Garlic Glazed Salmon

This Honey Garlic Glazed Salmon is sweet, savory, and full of flavor. It's an easy recipe that delivers restaurant-quality results at home.

TOTAL TIME COOKING: 20 minutes

Ingredients:

- 4 salmon fillets
- 3 tablespoons honey
- 2 tablespoons soy sauce
- 1 tablespoon lemon juice
- 3 cloves garlic, minced
- 1 tablespoon olive oil
- Salt and pepper, to taste

Directions:

1. In a small bowl, whisk together honey, soy sauce, lemon juice, and minced garlic.
2. Heat the olive oil in a large skillet over medium heat.

3. Season the salmon with salt and pepper, and place it in the skillet, skin-side down.
4. Cook for 3-4 minutes on each side until golden and cooked through.
5. Pour the honey garlic sauce over the salmon and cook for an additional 2 minutes, until the sauce is sticky and caramelized.
6. Serve with your favorite sides.

Baked Parmesan-Crusted Tilapia

This Baked Parmesan-Crusted Tilapia is crispy, flavorful, and incredibly easy to make. It's a great recipe for a quick and satisfying dinner.

TOTAL TIME COOKING: 25 minutes

Ingredients:

- 4 tilapia fillets
- 1/2 cup grated Parmesan cheese
- 1/4 cup breadcrumbs
- 2 tablespoons melted butter
- 1 teaspoon garlic powder
- Salt and pepper, to taste
- Lemon wedges, for serving

Directions:

1. Preheat your oven to 400°F (200°C) and line a baking sheet with parchment paper.
2. In a bowl, mix together Parmesan cheese, breadcrumbs, garlic powder, salt, and pepper.

3. Brush the tilapia fillets with melted butter and press them into the Parmesan mixture.
4. Place the fillets on the prepared baking sheet and bake for 10-12 minutes until golden brown.
5. Serve with lemon wedges and your favorite side dish.

Cajun Blackened Fish Tacos

These Cajun Blackened Fish T tacos are spicy, flavorful, and perfect for a quick dinner. They're easy to make and can be customized with your favorite toppings.

TOTAL TIME COOKING: 15 minutes

Ingredients:

- 4 white fish fillets (such as tilapia or cod)
- 2 tablespoons Cajun seasoning
- 2 tablespoons olive oil
- 8 small tortillas
- 1 cup shredded cabbage
- 1/2 cup salsa
- 1/4 cup sour cream
- Lime wedges, for serving

Directions:

1. Rub the fish fillets with Cajun seasoning.
2. Heat the olive oil in a large skillet over medium-high heat.

3. Cook the fish for 3-4 minutes on each side until blackened and cooked through.
4. Warm the tortillas in a dry skillet or microwave.
5. Assemble the tacos by placing the fish in the tortillas and topping with cabbage, salsa, and sour cream.
6. Serve with lime wedges.

Simple Baked Trout

This Simple Baked Trout is a no-fuss recipe that lets the natural flavor of the fish shine. It's perfect for a quick and healthy dinner.

TOTAL TIME COOKING: 25 minutes

Ingredients:

- 4 trout fillets
- 2 tablespoons olive oil
- 2 cloves garlic, minced
- Juice of 1 lemon
- 1 tablespoon fresh dill, chopped
- Salt and pepper, to taste

Directions:

1. Preheat your oven to 375°F (190°C) and line a baking sheet with parchment paper.
2. Place the trout fillets on the prepared baking sheet.
3. Drizzle with olive oil, and sprinkle with garlic, lemon juice, dill, salt, and pepper.

4. Bake for 15-18 minutes until the fish flakes easily with a fork.
5. Serve with your favorite side dishes.

Teriyaki Glazed Salmon

This Teriyaki Glazed Salmon is sweet, savory, and full of umami flavor. It's a quick and easy dish that pairs well with rice and steamed vegetables.

TOTAL TIME COOKING: 20 minutes

Ingredients:

- 4 salmon fillets
- 1/4 cup soy sauce
- 2 tablespoons honey
- 1 tablespoon rice vinegar
- 1 teaspoon sesame oil
- 1 tablespoon grated ginger
- 2 cloves garlic, minced
- 1 teaspoon cornstarch mixed with 1 tablespoon water

Directions:

1. In a small saucepan, combine soy sauce, honey, rice vinegar, sesame oil, ginger, and garlic. Bring to a simmer.

2. Stir in the cornstarch mixture and cook until the sauce thickens.
3. Preheat a large skillet over medium-high heat and cook the salmon fillets, skin-side down, for 3-4 minutes on each side.
4. Pour the teriyaki sauce over the salmon and cook for another minute, until glazed.
5. Serve with rice and steamed vegetables.

Quick Lemon Herb Grilled Swordfish

This Quick Lemon Herb Grilled Swordfish is simple yet flavorful. The lemon and herbs enhance the natural taste of the swordfish, making it a delicious and healthy meal.

TOTAL TIME COOKING: 15 minutes

Ingredients:

- 4 swordfish steaks
- 2 tablespoons olive oil
- Juice of 1 lemon
- 1 tablespoon fresh rosemary, chopped
- 1 tablespoon fresh thyme, chopped
- Salt and pepper, to taste

Directions:

1. Preheat your grill to medium-high heat.
2. In a small bowl, mix together olive oil, lemon juice, rosemary, thyme, salt, and pepper.
3. Brush the swordfish steaks with the lemon herb mixture.

4. Grill the swordfish for 4-5 minutes on each side, until cooked through.
5. Serve with a fresh salad or grilled vegetables.

Grilled Lemon Herb Salmon

Grilled Lemon Herb Salmon is a classic and simple dish that's perfect for any occasion. The lemon and fresh herbs enhance the natural flavors of the salmon, making it a healthy and delicious option.

TOTAL TIME COOKING: 15 minutes

Ingredients:

- 4 salmon fillets
- 2 tablespoons olive oil
- Juice of 1 lemon
- 1 tablespoon fresh dill, chopped
- 1 tablespoon fresh parsley, chopped
- Salt and pepper, to taste

Directions:

1. Preheat your grill to medium-high heat.
2. In a small bowl, mix together olive oil, lemon juice, dill, parsley, salt, and pepper.
3. Brush the salmon fillets with the lemon herb mixture.
4. Grill the salmon, skin-side down, for 4-5 minutes per side until the fish is cooked through and flakes easily.
5. Serve immediately with your favorite sides.

Grilled Cajun Tilapia

This Grilled Cajun Tilapia is full of bold flavors and is incredibly easy to prepare. The Cajun seasoning adds a spicy kick that pairs perfectly with the mild fish.

TOTAL TIME COOKING: 12 minutes

Ingredients:

- 4 tilapia fillets
- 2 tablespoons olive oil
- 2 tablespoons Cajun seasoning
- 1 lemon, cut into wedges

Directions:

1. Preheat your grill to medium-high heat.
2. Rub the tilapia fillets with olive oil and Cajun seasoning.
3. Grill the tilapia for 3-4 minutes on each side until the fish is opaque and flakes easily with a fork.
4. Serve with lemon wedges for squeezing over the fish.

Grilled Mahi Mahi with Mango Salsa

This Grilled Mahi Mahi with Mango Salsa is a tropical delight. The fresh mango salsa pairs perfectly with the firm, flavorful fish, making it a great dish for summer grilling.

TOTAL TIME COOKING: 20 minutes

Ingredients:

- 4 mahi mahi fillets
- 2 tablespoons olive oil
- 1 teaspoon ground cumin
- 1 teaspoon paprika
- Salt and pepper, to taste

Mango Salsa:

- 1 ripe mango, diced
- 1/4 red onion, finely chopped
- 1 jalapeño, seeded and finely chopped
- Juice of 1 lime
- 2 tablespoons fresh cilantro, chopped

Directions:

1. Preheat your grill to medium-high heat.
2. In a small bowl, mix together olive oil, cumin, paprika, salt, and pepper. Brush the mixture onto the mahi mahi fillets.
3. Grill the mahi mahi for 4-5 minutes on each side until cooked through.
4. While the fish is grilling, prepare the mango salsa by combining all the salsa ingredients in a bowl.
5. Serve the grilled mahi mahi topped with mango salsa.

Grilled Swordfish Steaks with Rosemary and Garlic

Grilled Swordfish Steaks with Rosemary and Garlic is a hearty and flavorful dish. The rosemary and garlic add depth to the swordfish, making it a satisfying meal for any occasion.

TOTAL TIME COOKING: 15 minutes

Ingredients:

- 4 swordfish steaks
- 2 tablespoons olive oil
- 2 cloves garlic, minced
- 1 tablespoon fresh rosemary, chopped
- Juice of 1 lemon
- Salt and pepper, to taste

Directions:

1. Preheat your grill to medium-high heat.
2. In a small bowl, mix together olive oil, garlic, rosemary, lemon juice, salt, and pepper.
3. Brush the mixture onto the swordfish steaks.

4. Grill the swordfish for 4-5 minutes on each side until the fish is cooked through and has nice grill marks.
5. Serve immediately with a side of grilled vegetables.

Grilled Tuna Steaks with Soy and Ginger

Grilled Tuna Steaks with Soy and Ginger is a quick and easy recipe that delivers big on flavor. The soy and ginger marinade gives the tuna a delicious Asian-inspired twist.

TOTAL TIME COOKING: 15 minutes

Ingredients:

- 4 tuna steaks
- 2 tablespoons soy sauce
- 1 tablespoon sesame oil
- 1 tablespoon fresh ginger, grated
- 2 cloves garlic, minced
- Juice of 1 lime

Directions:

1. In a small bowl, whisk together soy sauce, sesame oil, ginger, garlic, and lime juice.
2. Marinate the tuna steaks in the soy ginger mixture for 10 minutes.
3. Preheat your grill to high heat.

4. Grill the tuna steaks for 2-3 minutes on each side for medium-rare, or longer if desired.
5. Serve with a side of steamed rice or a fresh salad.

Grilled Halibut with Basil Pesto

Grilled Halibut with Basil Pesto is a light and flavorful dish that's perfect for summer. The basil pesto adds a fresh and aromatic touch to the firm, meaty halibut.

TOTAL TIME COOKING: 15 minutes

Ingredients:

- 4 halibut fillets
- 2 tablespoons olive oil
- Salt and pepper, to taste
- 1/4 cup basil pesto (store-bought or homemade)

Directions:

1. Preheat your grill to medium-high heat.
2. Brush the halibut fillets with olive oil and season with salt and pepper.
3. Grill the halibut for 4-5 minutes on each side until cooked through.
4. Top each fillet with a spoonful of basil pesto and serve immediately.

Grilled Trout with Lemon and Dill

Grilled Trout with Lemon and Dill is a simple and delicious dish that highlights the delicate flavor of the trout. The lemon and dill complement the fish perfectly, making it a refreshing and light meal.

TOTAL TIME COOKING: 20 minutes

Ingredients:

- 4 trout fillets
- 2 tablespoons olive oil
- Juice of 1 lemon
- 1 tablespoon fresh dill, chopped
- Salt and pepper, to taste

Directions:

1. Preheat your grill to medium-high heat.
2. Brush the trout fillets with olive oil and lemon juice, and season with dill, salt, and pepper.
3. Grill the trout for 5-6 minutes on each side until the fish is cooked through and flakes easily.
4. Serve with a side of grilled vegetables or a fresh salad.

Grilled Red Snapper with Garlic and Herbs

Grilled Red Snapper with Garlic and Herbs is a flavorful and healthy dish that's perfect for any occasion. The garlic and herbs enhance the natural taste of the red snapper, making it a delicious and easy meal.

TOTAL TIME COOKING: 15 minutes

Ingredients:

- 4 red snapper fillets
- 3 cloves garlic, minced
- 2 tablespoons olive oil
- 1 tablespoon fresh thyme, chopped
- 1 tablespoon fresh oregano, chopped
- Salt and pepper, to taste

Directions:

1. Preheat your grill to medium-high heat.
2. In a small bowl, mix together garlic, olive oil, thyme, oregano, salt, and pepper.
3. Brush the mixture onto the red snapper fillets.

4. Grill the red snapper for 4-5 minutes on each side until the fish is cooked through and has nice grill marks.
5. Serve immediately with a squeeze of fresh lemon juice.

Grilled Sea Bass with Lemon Garlic Sauce

Grilled Sea Bass with Lemon Garlic Sauce is a delicate and flavorful dish that's perfect for a special dinner. The lemon garlic sauce adds a bright and zesty flavor to the tender sea bass.

TOTAL TIME COOKING: 20 minutes

Ingredients:

- 4 sea bass fillets
- 2 tablespoons olive oil
- Juice of 1 lemon
- 3 cloves garlic, minced
- Salt and pepper, to taste
- Fresh parsley, chopped (optional)

Directions:

1. Preheat your grill to medium-high heat.
2. Brush the sea bass fillets with olive oil, and season with salt and pepper.

3. Grill the sea bass for 4-5 minutes on each side until cooked through.
4. In a small saucepan, heat the lemon juice and minced garlic over low heat.
5. Pour the lemon garlic sauce over the grilled sea bass and garnish with fresh parsley, if desired.
6. Serve with a side of grilled asparagus or steamed vegetables.

Classic Southern Fried Catfish

Classic Southern Fried Catfish is crispy on the outside and tender on the inside. This recipe is a staple in Southern cuisine and pairs perfectly with coleslaw and hush puppies.

TOTAL TIME COOKING: 20 minutes

Ingredients:

- 4 catfish fillets
- 1 cup cornmeal
- 1/2 cup all-purpose flour
- 1 teaspoon garlic powder
- 1 teaspoon paprika
- Salt and pepper, to taste
- 1 cup buttermilk
- Vegetable oil, for frying
- Lemon wedges, for serving

Directions:

1. In a shallow dish, mix together cornmeal, flour, garlic powder, paprika, salt, and pepper.

2. Pour the buttermilk into another shallow dish.
3. Dip each catfish fillet into the buttermilk, then dredge in the cornmeal mixture, coating evenly.
4. Heat about 1/2 inch of vegetable oil in a large skillet over medium-high heat.
5. Fry the catfish fillets for 3-4 minutes on each side until golden brown and crispy.
6. Drain on paper towels and serve with lemon wedges.

Crispy Fried Tilapia

Crispy Fried Tilapia is a quick and easy recipe that's perfect for a weeknight dinner. The light and crispy coating makes it a family favorite.

TOTAL TIME COOKING: 15 minutes

Ingredients:

- 4 tilapia fillets
- 1 cup all-purpose flour
- 2 eggs, beaten
- 1 cup breadcrumbs
- 1/2 teaspoon garlic powder
- 1/2 teaspoon onion powder
- Salt and pepper, to taste
- Vegetable oil, for frying
- Lemon wedges, for serving

Directions:

1. In three separate shallow dishes, place the flour, beaten eggs, and breadcrumbs.

2. Season the flour with garlic powder, onion powder, salt, and pepper.
3. Dredge each tilapia fillet in the flour, then dip into the beaten eggs, and finally coat with breadcrumbs.
4. Heat about 1/4 inch of vegetable oil in a large skillet over medium-high heat.
5. Fry the tilapia fillets for 3-4 minutes on each side until golden brown and crispy.
6. Drain on paper towels and serve with lemon wedges.

Beer-Battered Fish

Beer-Battered Fish is a pub favorite that you can easily make at home. The beer batter creates a light, crispy coating that's perfect for any white fish.

TOTAL TIME COOKING: 25 minutes

Ingredients:

- 4 white fish fillets (such as cod or haddock)
- 1 cup all-purpose flour
- 1 teaspoon baking powder
- 1/2 teaspoon salt
- 1/2 teaspoon paprika
- 1 cup cold beer
- Vegetable oil, for frying
- Tartar sauce, for serving

Directions:

1. In a large bowl, whisk together flour, baking powder, salt, and paprika.
2. Gradually add the cold beer, whisking until smooth.

3. Heat about 1 inch of vegetable oil in a deep skillet or pot over medium-high heat.
4. Dip each fish fillet into the beer batter, allowing excess to drip off.
5. Carefully place the battered fish into the hot oil and fry for 4-5 minutes, turning once, until golden brown and crispy.
6. Drain on paper towels and serve with tartar sauce.

Panko-Crusted Fried Cod

Panko-Crusted Fried Cod is a deliciously crispy dish that's quick to make. The panko breadcrumbs create a light and crunchy texture that pairs well with a squeeze of lemon.

TOTAL TIME COOKING: 20 minutes

Ingredients:

- 4 cod fillets
- 1 cup all-purpose flour
- 2 eggs, beaten
- 1 cup panko breadcrumbs
- 1/2 teaspoon garlic powder
- Salt and pepper, to taste
- Vegetable oil, for frying
- Lemon wedges, for serving

Directions:

1. In three separate shallow dishes, place the flour, beaten eggs, and panko breadcrumbs.
2. Season the flour with garlic powder, salt, and pepper.

3. Dredge each cod fillet in the flour, then dip into the beaten eggs, and finally coat with panko breadcrumbs.
4. Heat about 1/2 inch of vegetable oil in a large skillet over medium-high heat.
5. Fry the cod fillets for 3-4 minutes on each side until golden brown and crispy.
6. Drain on paper towels and serve with lemon wedges.

Fried Fish Tacos

Fried Fish Tacos are a delicious and fun way to enjoy fish. The crispy fried fish, combined with fresh toppings, makes for a perfect taco night.

TOTAL TIME COOKING: 20 minutes

Ingredients:

- 4 white fish fillets (such as tilapia or cod)
- 1 cup all-purpose flour
- 2 eggs, beaten
- 1 cup breadcrumbs
- 1/2 teaspoon cumin
- 1/2 teaspoon chili powder
- Salt and pepper, to taste
- Vegetable oil, for frying
- 8 small tortillas
- Shredded cabbage, salsa, and lime wedges, for serving

<u>Directions:</u>

1. In three separate shallow dishes, place the flour, beaten eggs, and breadcrumbs.
2. Season the flour with cumin, chili powder, salt, and pepper.
3. Dredge each fish fillet in the flour, then dip into the beaten eggs, and finally coat with breadcrumbs.
4. Heat about 1/4 inch of vegetable oil in a large skillet over medium-high heat.
5. Fry the fish fillets for 3-4 minutes on each side until golden brown and crispy.
6. Drain on paper towels and slice the fish into strips.
7. Warm the tortillas and assemble the tacos by placing the fried fish in the tortillas and topping with shredded cabbage, salsa, and a squeeze of lime.

Creamy Garlic Parmesan Fish

Creamy Garlic Parmesan Fish is a rich and flavorful dish that's perfect for a comforting meal. The creamy sauce, made with garlic and Parmesan, complements the tender fish beautifully.

TOTAL TIME COOKING: 20 minutes

Ingredients:

- 4 white fish fillets (such as tilapia or cod)
- 2 tablespoons butter
- 3 cloves garlic, minced
- 1 cup heavy cream
- 1/2 cup grated Parmesan cheese
- 1 tablespoon fresh parsley, chopped
- Salt and pepper, to taste

Directions:

1. Season the fish fillets with salt and pepper.
2. In a large skillet, melt the butter over medium heat.

3. Add the fish fillets and cook for 3-4 minutes on each side until golden and cooked through. Remove from the skillet and set aside.
4. In the same skillet, add the minced garlic and cook for 1 minute until fragrant.
5. Pour in the heavy cream and bring to a simmer, then stir in the Parmesan cheese until the sauce thickens.
6. Return the fish to the skillet, spoon the sauce over the fillets, and cook for an additional 2 minutes.
7. Garnish with fresh parsley and serve immediately.

Tomato Basil Fish

Tomato Basil Fish is a light and fresh dish that's full of Mediterranean flavors. The combination of tomatoes, basil, and garlic creates a delicious sauce that pairs perfectly with the fish.

TOTAL TIME COOKING: 25 minutes

Ingredients:

- 4 white fish fillets (such as cod or haddock)
- 2 tablespoons olive oil
- 1 onion, finely chopped
- 3 cloves garlic, minced
- 1 can (14 oz) diced tomatoes
- 1/4 cup fresh basil, chopped
- Salt and pepper, to taste
- Lemon wedges, for serving

Directions:

1. Heat the olive oil in a large skillet over medium heat.
2. Add the chopped onion and cook until softened.

3. Stir in the minced garlic and cook for 1 minute.
4. Add the diced tomatoes and bring the mixture to a simmer. Cook for 5-7 minutes until the sauce thickens slightly.
5. Season the fish fillets with salt and pepper, then place them in the skillet, spooning some sauce over the top.
6. Cover and cook for 8-10 minutes, or until the fish is cooked through.
7. Sprinkle with fresh basil and serve with lemon wedges.

Coconut Curry Fish

Coconut Curry Fish is a flavorful and aromatic dish inspired by Indian cuisine. The creamy coconut curry sauce is infused with spices, making it a delicious and satisfying meal.

TOTAL TIME COOKING: 30 minutes

Ingredients:

- 4 white fish fillets (such as tilapia or snapper)
- 1 tablespoon vegetable oil
- 1 onion, finely chopped
- 2 cloves garlic, minced
- 1 tablespoon curry powder
- 1 can (14 oz) coconut milk
- 1 can (14 oz) diced tomatoes, drained
- Salt and pepper, to taste
- Fresh cilantro, chopped (optional)

Directions:

1. Heat the vegetable oil in a large skillet over medium heat.

2. Add the chopped onion and cook until softened.
3. Stir in the minced garlic and curry powder, cooking for 1 minute until fragrant.
4. Pour in the coconut milk and diced tomatoes, stirring to combine.
5. Bring the mixture to a simmer, then add the fish fillets. Season with salt and pepper.
6. Cover and cook for 10-12 minutes until the fish is cooked through and flakes easily.
7. Garnish with fresh cilantro, if desired, and serve with rice.

Lemon Butter Fish

Lemon Butter Fish is a simple and elegant dish that's quick to prepare. The lemon butter sauce adds a bright, tangy flavor that complements the delicate fish perfectly.

TOTAL TIME COOKING: 15 minutes

Ingredients:

- 4 white fish fillets (such as cod or sole)
- 2 tablespoons butter
- Juice of 1 lemon
- 2 cloves garlic, minced
- 1 tablespoon fresh parsley, chopped
- Salt and pepper, to taste

Directions:

1. Season the fish fillets with salt and pepper.
2. In a large skillet, melt the butter over medium heat.

3. Add the fish fillets and cook for 3-4 minutes on each side until golden and cooked through. Remove from the skillet and set aside.
4. In the same skillet, add the minced garlic and cook for 1 minute until fragrant.
5. Stir in the lemon juice and cook for an additional minute.
6. Return the fish to the skillet, spoon the lemon butter sauce over the fillets, and cook for another 2 minutes.
7. Garnish with fresh parsley and serve immediately.

Dijon Mustard Cream Fish

Dijon Mustard Cream Fish is a rich and tangy dish that's easy to make. The creamy Dijon mustard sauce pairs beautifully with the mild fish, creating a delicious and satisfying meal.

TOTAL TIME COOKING: 20 minutes

Ingredients:

- 4 white fish fillets (such as halibut or haddock)
- 2 tablespoons butter
- 2 tablespoons Dijon mustard
- 1/2 cup heavy cream
- 1 tablespoon fresh dill, chopped
- Salt and pepper, to taste

Directions:

1. Season the fish fillets with salt and pepper.
2. In a large skillet, melt the butter over medium heat.

3. Add the fish fillets and cook for 3-4 minutes on each side until golden and cooked through. Remove from the skillet and set aside.
4. In the same skillet, whisk together the Dijon mustard and heavy cream, bringing the mixture to a simmer.
5. Stir in the fresh dill and cook for 2-3 minutes until the sauce thickens slightly.
6. Return the fish to the skillet, spoon the Dijon cream sauce over the fillets, and cook for another 2 minutes.
7. Serve immediately with your favorite sides.

Stuffed Salmon with Spinach and Cream Cheese

Stuffed Salmon with Spinach and Cream Cheese is a rich and flavorful dish that's surprisingly easy to make. The creamy filling adds a delicious contrast to the tender, flaky salmon.

TOTAL TIME COOKING: 30 minutes

Ingredients:

- 4 salmon fillets
- 4 oz cream cheese, softened
- 1 cup fresh spinach, chopped
- 1/2 teaspoon garlic powder
- 1/2 teaspoon onion powder
- Salt and pepper, to taste
- 1 tablespoon olive oil
- Lemon wedges, for serving

Directions:

1. Preheat your oven to 375°F (190°C).

2. In a bowl, mix together the cream cheese, chopped spinach, garlic powder, onion powder, salt, and pepper.
3. Cut a slit along the side of each salmon fillet to create a pocket.
4. Stuff the spinach and cream cheese mixture into the pockets.
5. Heat the olive oil in an oven-safe skillet over medium heat.
6. Sear the salmon fillets for 2-3 minutes on each side until golden brown.
7. Transfer the skillet to the preheated oven and bake for 10-12 minutes, or until the salmon is cooked through.
8. Serve with lemon wedges.

Crab-Stuffed Flounder

Crab-Stuffed Flounder is a decadent dish that's perfect for a special occasion. The sweet crab meat and buttery flounder make a delightful pairing.

TOTAL TIME COOKING: 35 minutes

Ingredients:

- 4 flounder fillets
- 1/2 lb crab meat
- 1/4 cup breadcrumbs
- 1/4 cup mayonnaise
- 1 tablespoon Dijon mustard
- 1 tablespoon lemon juice
- 1 tablespoon fresh parsley, chopped
- Salt and pepper, to taste
- 2 tablespoons butter, melted

Directions:

1. Preheat your oven to 350°F (175°C).

2. In a bowl, combine the crab meat, breadcrumbs, mayonnaise, Dijon mustard, lemon juice, parsley, salt, and pepper.
3. Place the flounder fillets on a baking sheet.
4. Spoon the crab mixture onto one side of each fillet, then fold the other side over the filling.
5. Brush the tops with melted butter.
6. Bake for 20-25 minutes until the flounder is cooked through and the crab stuffing is golden.

Stuffed Trout with Lemon and Herbs

Stuffed Trout with Lemon and Herbs is a light and fresh dish that's full of flavor. The combination of herbs, garlic, and lemon gives the trout a bright, zesty taste.

TOTAL TIME COOKING: 25 minutes

Ingredients:

- 4 whole trout, cleaned and gutted
- 2 lemons, thinly sliced
- 4 cloves garlic, minced
- 1/4 cup fresh parsley, chopped
- 1/4 cup fresh dill, chopped
- Salt and pepper, to taste
- 2 tablespoons olive oil

Directions:

1. Preheat your oven to 375°F (190°C).
2. In a bowl, mix together the minced garlic, parsley, dill, salt, and pepper.
3. Stuff each trout with the herb mixture and lemon slices.

4. Place the stuffed trout on a baking sheet and drizzle with olive oil.
5. Bake for 15-20 minutes until the trout is cooked through and flaky.
6. Serve with additional lemon wedges.

Shrimp-Stuffed Tilapia

Shrimp-Stuffed Tilapia is a deliciously elegant dish that's perfect for impressing guests. The shrimp stuffing is savory and complements the mild tilapia perfectly.

TOTAL TIME COOKING: 30 minutes

Ingredients:

- 4 tilapia fillets
- 1/2 lb shrimp, peeled, deveined, and chopped
- 1/4 cup breadcrumbs
- 2 tablespoons mayonnaise
- 1 tablespoon lemon juice
- 1 teaspoon Old Bay seasoning
- 1 tablespoon fresh parsley, chopped
- Salt and pepper, to taste

Directions:

1. Preheat your oven to 375°F (190°C).
2. In a bowl, combine the chopped shrimp, breadcrumbs, mayonnaise, lemon juice, Old Bay seasoning, parsley, salt, and pepper.

3. Place the tilapia fillets on a baking sheet.
4. Spoon the shrimp mixture onto one side of each fillet, then fold the other side over the filling.
5. Bake for 20-25 minutes until the tilapia is cooked through and the shrimp stuffing is golden.
6. Serve immediately with a side of steamed vegetables or rice.

Stuffed Haddock with Spinach and Feta

Stuffed Haddock with Spinach and Feta is a flavorful and healthy dish that's easy to prepare. The spinach and feta stuffing adds a tangy and savory element to the mild haddock.

TOTAL TIME COOKING: 35 minutes

Ingredients:

- 4 haddock fillets
- 1 cup fresh spinach, chopped
- 1/2 cup feta cheese, crumbled
- 1/4 cup breadcrumbs
- 1 clove garlic, minced
- 1 tablespoon olive oil
- Salt and pepper, to taste
- Lemon wedges, for serving

Directions:

1. Preheat your oven to 375°F (190°C).

2. In a bowl, mix together the chopped spinach, feta cheese, breadcrumbs, minced garlic, olive oil, salt, and pepper.
3. Cut a slit along the side of each haddock fillet to create a pocket.
4. Stuff the spinach and feta mixture into the pockets.
5. Place the stuffed haddock on a baking sheet and drizzle with a little olive oil.
6. Bake for 20-25 minutes until the haddock is cooked through and the stuffing is golden.

Steamed Ginger Soy Snapper

Steamed Ginger Soy Snapper is a delicate and healthy dish that highlights the natural flavors of fresh fish. The aromatic ginger and savory soy sauce create a simple yet sophisticated meal.

TOTAL TIME COOKING: 25 minutes

Ingredients:

- 1 whole red snapper (about 2 lbs), cleaned and scaled
- 2 inches fresh ginger, julienned
- 4 green onions, sliced into thin strips
- 1/4 cup soy sauce
- 2 tablespoons rice vinegar
- 1 tablespoon sesame oil
- 2 tablespoons vegetable oil
- 1 red chili, sliced (optional)
- Fresh cilantro, for garnish

Directions:

1. Prepare a large steamer or set up a makeshift steamer using a wok and a steaming rack.

2. Place the cleaned snapper on a heatproof plate that fits inside your steamer. Scatter half of the ginger and green onions over and inside the fish.
3. Place the plate inside the steamer and steam over boiling water for 15-18 minutes, or until the fish flakes easily with a fork.
4. In a small bowl, combine soy sauce and rice vinegar. Set aside.
5. Once the fish is cooked, carefully remove it from the steamer. Discard any accumulated liquid on the plate.
6. Scatter the remaining ginger, green onions, and red chili over the fish.
7. Heat sesame oil and vegetable oil in a small saucepan until hot. Carefully pour the hot oil over the fish to cook the aromatics slightly.
8. Drizzle the soy sauce mixture over the fish and garnish with fresh cilantro. Serve immediately with steamed rice.

Maple Glazed Salmon

Maple Glazed Salmon is a sweet and savory dish that brings out the natural richness of the salmon. The combination of maple syrup and Dijon mustard creates a delicious glaze that caramelizes perfectly when cooked.

TOTAL TIME COOKING: 20 minutes

Ingredients:

- 4 salmon fillets
- 1/4 cup maple syrup
- 2 tablespoons Dijon mustard
- 1 tablespoon soy sauce
- 1 clove garlic, minced
- Salt and pepper, to taste

Directions:

1. Preheat your oven to 400°F (200°C).
2. In a small bowl, whisk together the maple syrup, Dijon mustard, soy sauce, minced garlic, salt, and pepper.
3. Place the salmon fillets on a baking sheet lined with parchment paper.
4. Brush the maple glaze over the salmon fillets.

5. Bake for 12-15 minutes, or until the salmon is cooked through and the glaze is caramelized.
6. Serve with steamed vegetables or rice.

Pistachio-Crusted Cod

Pistachio-Crusted Cod is a unique and crunchy dish that pairs the mild flavor of cod with the nutty taste of pistachios. This recipe is simple yet impressive, perfect for a special dinner.

TOTAL TIME COOKING: 25 minutes

Ingredients:

- 4 cod fillets
- 1/2 cup pistachios, finely chopped
- 1/4 cup breadcrumbs
- 2 tablespoons olive oil
- 1 tablespoon Dijon mustard
- Salt and pepper, to taste

Directions:

1. Preheat your oven to 375°F (190°C).
2. In a small bowl, mix together the chopped pistachios, breadcrumbs, olive oil, salt, and pepper.
3. Brush each cod fillet with Dijon mustard, then press the pistachio mixture onto the fillets.

4. Place the cod on a baking sheet and bake for 15-18 minutes, or until the fish is cooked through and the crust is golden.
5. Serve with a side salad or roasted vegetables.

Moroccan Spiced Fish

Moroccan Spiced Fish is a bold and aromatic dish that brings the flavors of North Africa to your table. The combination of spices and citrus creates a unique and flavorful meal.

TOTAL TIME COOKING: 25 minutes

Ingredients:

- 4 white fish fillets (such as tilapia or cod)
- 1 teaspoon ground cumin
- 1 teaspoon ground coriander
- 1/2 teaspoon ground paprika
- 1/2 teaspoon ground cinnamon
- 1/4 teaspoon cayenne pepper
- Juice of 1 lemon
- 2 tablespoons olive oil
- Salt and pepper, to taste

Directions:

1. In a small bowl, mix together cumin, coriander, paprika, cinnamon, cayenne pepper, salt, and pepper.

2. Rub the spice mixture onto both sides of the fish fillets.
3. Heat the olive oil in a large skillet over medium heat.
4. Cook the fish fillets for 3-4 minutes on each side until cooked through.
5. Squeeze lemon juice over the fish and serve with couscous or a fresh salad.

Grilled Fish Tacos with Avocado Crema

Grilled Fish Tacos with Avocado Crema are a fun and fresh dish that's perfect for a casual meal. The grilled fish pairs perfectly with the creamy avocado sauce, making these tacos irresistible.

TOTAL TIME COOKING: 20 minutes

Ingredients:

- 4 white fish fillets (such as tilapia or cod)
- 1 tablespoon olive oil
- 1 teaspoon chili powder
- 1/2 teaspoon cumin
- 1/2 teaspoon garlic powder
- Salt and pepper, to taste
- 8 small tortillas
- 1 avocado
- 1/4 cup sour cream
- Juice of 1 lime
- Fresh cilantro, chopped

Directions:

1. Preheat your grill to medium-high heat.

2. In a small bowl, mix together olive oil, chili powder, cumin, garlic powder, salt, and pepper. Brush the mixture onto the fish fillets.
3. Grill the fish for 3-4 minutes on each side until cooked through.
4. While the fish is grilling, mash the avocado and mix with sour cream, lime juice, and cilantro to make the avocado crema.
5. Warm the tortillas and assemble the tacos by placing the grilled fish in the tortillas and topping with avocado crema and extra cilantro.
6. Serve with lime wedges.

Lemon Basil Baked Fish

Lemon Basil Baked Fish is a simple and fresh dish that's full of flavor. The lemon and basil give the fish a light and fragrant taste, making it a perfect meal for any time of the year.

TOTAL TIME COOKING: 20 minutes

Ingredients:

- 4 white fish fillets (such as cod or halibut)
- 2 tablespoons olive oil
- Juice of 1 lemon
- 1/4 cup fresh basil, chopped
- 1 clove garlic, minced
- Salt and pepper, to taste

Directions:

1. Preheat your oven to 375°F (190°C).
2. In a small bowl, mix together olive oil, lemon juice, basil, garlic, salt, and pepper.
3. Place the fish fillets in a baking dish and pour the lemon basil mixture over them.
4. Bake for 12-15 minutes, or until the fish is cooked through.

Ginger Scallion Steamed Fish

Ginger Scallion Steamed Fish is a classic Chinese dish known for its light, delicate flavors. The combination of fresh ginger and scallions enhances the natural taste of the fish, making it a healthy and delicious option.

TOTAL TIME COOKING: 20 minutes

Ingredients:

- 4 white fish fillets (such as tilapia or cod)
- 2 tablespoons soy sauce
- 2 tablespoons sesame oil
- 2-inch piece of fresh ginger, julienned
- 4 scallions, cut into thin strips
- 1 tablespoon rice vinegar
- Fresh cilantro, chopped (optional)

Directions:

1. Place the fish fillets on a heatproof plate that fits into your steamer basket.
2. Top the fish with the julienned ginger and scallions.
3. In a small bowl, mix together the soy sauce, sesame oil, and rice vinegar.

4. Pour the sauce over the fish fillets.
5. Steam the fish over boiling water for 10-12 minutes, or until the fish is cooked through and flakes easily with a fork.
6. Garnish with fresh cilantro if desired and serve immediately.

Steamed Fish with Lemon and Herbs

Steamed Fish with Lemon and Herbs is a simple and fragrant dish that's perfect for a light meal. The lemon and fresh herbs infuse the fish with a bright, refreshing flavor.

TOTAL TIME COOKING: 20 minutes

Ingredients:

- 4 white fish fillets (such as cod or halibut)
- 1 lemon, thinly sliced
- 2 tablespoons fresh parsley, chopped
- 1 tablespoon fresh dill, chopped
- 1 tablespoon olive oil
- Salt and pepper, to taste

Directions:

1. Place the fish fillets on a heatproof plate that fits into your steamer basket.
2. Top the fish with lemon slices, parsley, dill, salt, and pepper.
3. Drizzle with olive oil.

4. Steam the fish over boiling water for 10-12 minutes, or until the fish is cooked through and flakes easily with a fork.
5. Serve with additional lemon wedges and your favorite side dish.

Thai-Style Steamed Fish

Thai-Style Steamed Fish is a flavorful dish that combines the heat of chili with the freshness of lime and cilantro. It's a quick and easy recipe that's packed with vibrant flavors.

TOTAL TIME COOKING: 20 minutes

Ingredients:

- 4 white fish fillets (such as snapper or tilapia)
- 2 cloves garlic, minced
- 1 red chili, thinly sliced
- 2 tablespoons fish sauce
- Juice of 1 lime
- 1 tablespoon soy sauce
- 1 tablespoon brown sugar
- Fresh cilantro, chopped

Directions:

1. Place the fish fillets on a heatproof plate that fits into your steamer basket.
2. In a small bowl, mix together the garlic, red chili, fish sauce, lime juice, soy sauce, and brown sugar.
3. Pour the sauce over the fish fillets.

4. Steam the fish over boiling water for 10-12 minutes, or until the fish is cooked through and flakes easily with a fork.
5. Garnish with fresh cilantro and serve with jasmine rice.

Mediterranean Steamed Fish

Mediterranean Steamed Fish is a light and healthy dish that's full of vibrant flavors. The combination of tomatoes, olives, and capers gives the fish a fresh and tangy taste.

TOTAL TIME COOKING: 25 minutes

Ingredients:

- 4 white fish fillets (such as cod or haddock)
- 1 cup cherry tomatoes, halved
- 1/4 cup black olives, pitted and sliced
- 2 tablespoons capers, rinsed
- 2 cloves garlic, minced
- 1 tablespoon olive oil
- Juice of 1 lemon
- Salt and pepper, to taste

Directions:

1. Place the fish fillets on a heatproof plate that fits into your steamer basket.
2. In a bowl, combine cherry tomatoes, olives, capers, garlic, olive oil, lemon juice, salt, and pepper.

3. Spoon the tomato mixture over the fish fillets.
4. Steam the fish over boiling water for 12-15 minutes, or until the fish is cooked through and flakes easily with a fork.
5. Serve with a side of couscous or a fresh salad.

Steamed Fish with Soy and Garlic

Steamed Fish with Soy and Garlic is a quick and easy dish that's full of savory flavors. The soy sauce and garlic create a simple yet delicious sauce that pairs perfectly with steamed fish.

TOTAL TIME COOKING: 20 minutes

Ingredients:

- 4 white fish fillets (such as tilapia or sea bass)
- 2 tablespoons soy sauce
- 2 cloves garlic, minced
- 1 tablespoon sesame oil
- 1 tablespoon rice vinegar
- 1 teaspoon sugar
- 2 scallions, thinly sliced

Directions:

1. Place the fish fillets on a heatproof plate that fits into your steamer basket.
2. In a small bowl, mix together soy sauce, garlic, sesame oil, rice vinegar, and sugar.
3. Pour the sauce over the fish fillets.

4. Steam the fish over boiling water for 10-12 minutes, or until the fish is cooked through and flakes easily with a fork.
5. Garnish with sliced scallions and serve with steamed rice or vegetables.

Made in the USA
Monee, IL
16 April 2025